PAIGE WILEY AND LUKE BOBO

WORKED
UP NAVIGATING CALLING
AFTER COLLEGE

ISBN 9781697358841

Creative Direction: Eric Rivier
Cover Design: Gabriel Reyes-Ordeix and Eric Rivier
Interior Design: Gabriel Reyes-Ordeix

Printed in the United States of America
First Edition

Table of Contents

Intro-
duction

College can sometimes feel like repeating middle school. It's an exciting and unsettling time - one that often leads (even in all of its awkwardness) to great personal growth and change. But unlike the transition from middle school to high school, where you follow a carefully crafted schedule of classes and extracurriculars, graduating college often doesn't provide the clarity we hoped it would. Questions about your future loom in your mind and, most likely, keep you up at night. Maybe you have figured out your career path and are wondering how your faith fits into your new nine-to-five. Or maybe you graduated with a degree and can't determine the best next step to move forward in life and work. Wherever you find yourself, know you are not alone. The process of career development and decision making is a life-long journey. This is a pivotal season for you, but we hope this book reminds you that your career choices are never determinative of your identity, worth, or even the foreseeable future. The world wants us to believe that who we are is directly tied to a job, paycheck, or status, but as Christians we know who we already are in Christ. This brings freedom and, yes, a sigh of relief to your school weary soul. We believe God calls each of us to move forward in life in wisdom, faithfulness, and with our eyes open to the needs around us and how we can meet those in ways he has gifted us to in each season. As you work through this book, we pray your soul is encouraged more than anything. And, if you figure out what you want to do with your life, that's an added bonus. We are all becoming who God made us to be. And yes, he will use your career to shape who you are and love the world, but first there is grace to rest in the freedom of our identity in Christ before any other.

The Big Story

LUKE BOBO

creation
(how life *ought* to be) ———————

the fall
(how life *is*) ———————

redemption
(how life *can* be) ———————

consummation
(how life *will* be) ———————

"Daddy, Daddy,

tell me a story."

These were the words of

my daughter when

she was a child.

Why was my daughter

so intrigued by stories?

She knew we are wired

for stories.

Filmmakers know this.

Musicians know this.

God, the great storyteller,

knows this. What matters is

the story we live by

and Christians live by

the big story.

Believe it or not, each of these grand acts informs our daily work, our primary calling, and our many secondary callings.

creation ———— During this opening act recorded in Genesis 1-2, we are introduced to God as a diligent, thoughtful, and conscientious worker. We know God was engaged in work because of Genesis 2:1-3. In this short passage, we see the word "work" three times. Later, of course, in the biblical story we see God incarnate, Jesus, making tables and chairs in Joseph's carpentry shop. God values work.

As God's image bearers, we reflect his character by writing a good paper, caring for an elderly parent, and by exercising our duty to vote (Gen 1:26-28). And we reflect God by resting from our work (Gen 2:1-3). God models a working and resting rhythm worth imitating.

the fall ———— Act two introduces an unwelcome parasite[2] into God's creation: sin. From the beginning, sin has distorted relationships: God to humanity, person to person, our relationship with ourselves, the animal kingdom, creation, and men and women to their work. Work is still inherently good, but now there is sinful work and an unpleasant side of work. Work is now riddled with real frustration, heartache, and toil (Gen 3:17-19).

Sometimes work will be accompanied by tears and anxiety. Sometimes we will find our identity or worth in our work; in other words, sometimes we make work — something good — into the ultimate good. Work was never designed as the "be all, end all."

redemption ———— Redemption puts work and all vocations or callings into their proper perspective. Act three teaches us that our primary calling is to Christ alone. Os Guinness beautifully expounds, "Our primary calling as followers of Christ is by him, to him, and for him. First and foremost, we are called to Someone (God), not something (such as motherhood, politics, or teaching) or to somewhere (such as the inner city or Outer Mongolia)."[3] All Christians share this primary calling (or vocation).

All remaining callings (vocations) are secondary — being a worker, parent, citizen, caregiver, spouse. Christians do not share all secondary callings in common. For instance, God will call some to singleness and some to marriage. Secondary callings are fluid; our primary calling is not.

Work done well honors the Lord and serves as a means to worship God. Worship is not just reserved for when the church gathers. As we scatter to our places of work, engaging in our work gives us an opportunity to offer it to the Lord (Col 3:23-25).

consummation ———— Consummation marks the end of human history and, most importantly, the arrival of our king, where all the kingdoms of this world will be directly under the rule of God on earth (Rev 11:15). Consummation also marks the renewal of all things (Rev 21). As Amy Sherman explains, "God will make all things new and not make new things." In other words, we will work anew in the new heavens and new earth. Our work will be free of ungodly motives; our workplaces will be free of corruption, greed, and backstabbing. Our work will be free of frustration. We will delight in our assigned work in God's beautiful city.

So what does the end of the story have to do with our present reality? How can we each bring beauty and restoration to our workplaces?

Allow what will be true at the end of the story to inform your work week — Jesus will reign and make all things new. Our work and mere presence in our workplaces should be forestastes of the new heavens and new earth.

[1] Vincent Bacote, "The Goodness of Work," in *Whatever You do: Six Foundations for An Integrated Life* (Made to Flourish, 2019), 73.
[2] Cornelius Plantinga, *A Breviary of Sin: The Way It's Not Supposed To Be* (Grand Rapids: Eerdmans, 1995) 89.
[3] Os Guinness, *The Call: Finding and Fulfilling the Central Purpose of Your Life* (Nashville: W. Publishing Group, 2003) 31.

notes

What perspective does the four-act story give us about God as a worker? What does this tell us about the nature and value of our work?

"In the narrative of Genesis, God's image and likeness are closely connected to God's working.

This is confirmed by the first commandment given to God's image bearers: 'Be fruitful and multiply, and fill the earth and subdue it; and have dominion . . .' (Gen 1:28). Notice God's first instruction to human beings was not 'Build an altar,' 'Think rationally,' or even 'Love the Lord.' Rather, God told the beings created in God's own image to get to work."

Mark D. Roberts
"Faith and Work Integration:
Trendy or Essential?"

Dispelling Myths

PAIGE WILEY

"Myth has at least an imaginative outline of truth."
—G.K. Chesterton

In God's big story, we come to understand work is good. It's a part of the original (and perfect) design, and it's one of the primary ways we reflect God as his image bearers (imago Dei).

However, other stories compete for our attention. Our culture, families, churches, and peers all offer a variety of narratives about work. Unfortunately, many of these narratives have become distorted, and if you shape your life around these narratives, you will find more emptiness than fulfillment. Let's dive into some of these myths, and reorient ourselves to see things the way God sees them. We can all agree: Work needs a new story.

MYTH ONE

Work is a necessary evil.

When we talk about work, there's often what feels like a tangible gloom that hangs overhead. It's the "TGIF" motto or the "I Hate Mondays" t-shirts that drive a belief that work is, by nature, difficult, depressing, and unfulfilling. It's an annoying obstacle on our way to the weekend, and no trendy co-working space can convince us otherwise. Sure, it pays the bills and keeps food on the table, but other than that, we could do without it.

This belief doesn't stop at the cubicles of the modern office. Unfortunately, this sentiment has influenced teachings from the pulpit, too. Genesis 3:17-19 often inaccurately takes the main stage as the primary framework for why we work:

> To Adam [God] said, "Because you listened to your wife and ate from the tree about which I commanded you, 'You must not eat of it.' Cursed is the ground because of you; through painful toil you will eat of it all of the days of your life. It will produce thorns and thistles for you, and you will eat your food until you return to the ground, since from it you were taken; for dust you are and to dust you will return."

It's no wonder our own work mirrors the difficulty this passage describes. When most Christians talk about work, it's usually in this same, despairing way our colleagues and co-workers describe it. Work is toilsome. Work is tiresome. We sludge through in order to provide for our families and, if we're Christian, maybe witness to our coworkers.

But there's more to this story. Scripture is not inaccurate, but when read in isolation, it's incomplete.

This passage of Scripture is not inaccurate, but when we build our framework from Genesis 3 alone, we miss God's original intention for our work. When we start the story with the fall, it's like walking into a movie 20 minutes late, and the disorientation frustrates and confuses us.

So let's back up, starting our story with creation in Genesis 1:26-28:

> Then God said, "Let us make man in our image, in our likeness, and let them rule over the fish of the sea and the birds of the air, over the livestock, over all the earth, and over all the creatures that move along the ground." So God created man in his own image, in the image of God he created him; male and female, he created them. God blessed them and said to them, 'Be fruitful and increase in number; fill the earth and subdue it. Rule over the fish of the sea and the birds of the air and over every living creature that moves on the ground.

This is often called our cultural mandate — God giving us a whole Earth full of good ingredients. What he made he called "good," and he gave us the opportunity to continue stewarding that goodness. It's a wonderful invitation to joyfully co-create and cultivate these ingredients — wood to furniture, clay to pottery, language to song. God designed work to be part of our image-bearing. Our imago Dei. A beautiful gift and sacred responsibility from our creator. Work was part of the first act of the story; life before the fall.

If this is true, let's reframe why we work. Work is cursed, but it is not a curse. Work is meant to give us purpose and meaning. It is a unique way we get to create and cultivate the world with the ultimate and perfect creator and curator. If we view this blessing as a curse, our work will show it. But if we understand what work was intended to be in the beginning, it will inform how we work in a world longing to be cultivated, restored, and renewed.

MYTH TWO

My work defines my worth.

The world holds two extreme beliefs when it comes to work: Work means nothing or it means everything. The former group of people use work solely as a means to pay the bills, and are often disengaged from the purpose of their day-to-day jobs. The latter group, growing in number, elevate work as a primary source of purpose, identity, and calling. This newly practiced religion called "workism" moves the heart to make work — meant to be a good thing — an ultimate thing.

Although golden calves aren't (usually) present in the practice of workism, this religion offers a modern expression of idolatry. The Western world has seen a recent surge of this second group, reflecting a culture that longs to worship something, especially in the context of a societal decline of religious experiences.[4] This does not point to a decline in worship, but a shift in where and what we worship.

Elevating work to an improper place is not new (remember the Tower of Babel), but it is potentially more tempting than it has ever been. In a culture that praises hustle, productivity, and #nodaysoff, it can be tempting to fall into the mindset that work equals worth.

So what is the gospel response to this?

Work in itself is not evil. It's also not that God wants us to sit and home and avoid making work an idol. The problem is when we place our love for work before our love for God. It's when work is elevated to our primary identity instead of one of our secondary callings.

So how do we put work in its proper place? Here are a few action steps to consider:

thank God for your work ———

Thanking God for your ability to do the work you love is one way to remember work is a gift. When you take the time to remember the skills and talents you've been given — and who gave them to you — it will reorient you to remember why you work: to love God and to reflect his image in the good gifts he gives you.

pray over your work ———

Do you pray for your work? Not just for patience with frustrating coworkers or unwanted tasks, but for the health, goodness, and flourishing of your company and community? God promises to give wisdom to anyone who seeks it (Jas 1:5). Why not apply this to the wisdom of the actions, choices, and decisions of your workplace? This not only allows you to practice submission to God's presence at your company, but it serves as a reminder that God cares about and controls the mundane, the technical, and the complex pieces of our lives and work.

establish healthy boundaries ———

Like any healthy relationship, it's critical to set boundaries in order to flourish. If the temptation to overwork or indulge in a coworker's praise prevent you from loving God first, take some time to formulate healthy boundaries between you and your work. This may mean working fewer hours or taking on projects in secrecy, and it may be hard at first to implement these ideas. However, try to center yourself on the promise that God provides, and rewards those who earnestly seek him (Heb 11:6).

MYTH THREE

There is only one "right" career path for me.

During most of our young lives, we parallel the search for a career to the search for a soulmate. There is one "right" fit for us, and the remaining paths are diverging, deceptive roads to God's will for our lives. Whether intrinsically or extrinsically said, these messages infiltrate our culture, with an increasing sense of urgency and worry for picking the "right" option with bullseye-targeted accuracy.

I'd love to hand you some truth.

God is not playing games with you. He's not sneaky, and he's not absent if you aren't receiving a specific call or instruction. Instead, he is giving you freedom. He is giving you an opportunity to step out in faith. I love the way Kevin DeYoung puts it in his book, *Just Do Something*, when it comes to making critical life decisions:

> Go get a job, provided it's not wicked. ... But put aside the passivity and the quest for complete fulfillment and the perfectionism and the preoccupation with the future, and for God's sake start making some decisions in your life. Don't wait for the liver-shiver. If you are seeking first the kingdom of God and His righteousness, you will be in God's will, so just go out and do something.[5]

Some of us will get a "burning bush" moment. Like Moses, some of us will be called by God to specific missions, places, or job positions. And on the other hand, some of us won't. Some of us get the opportunity to use wisdom, trust, and intuition to guide the choices we face. And that's also a blessing.

God is a personal and persistent Father; therefore I humbly believe he offers wisdom and instruction when necessary. But sometimes there's no right or wrong answer. Sometimes he just wants you to do something! As long as you're in humble communion with God, pressing in, seeking wisdom, and answering your primary calling, you are within the context of his will.

[4] Derek Thompson, "Workism Is Making Americans Miserable," *The Atlantic*, March 05, 2019. Accessed April 08, 2019. https://www.theatlantic.com/ideas/archive/2019/02/religion-workism-making-americans-miserable/583441/.
[5] Kevin DeYoung, *Just Do Something: A Liberating Approach to Finding God's Will* (Chicago: Moody Publishers, 2014).

God is not playing games with you. He's not sneaky, and he's not absent if you aren't receiving a specific call or instruction. Instead, he is giving you freedom.

MYTH FOUR

If I'm serious about my faith, I need to consider doing global missions or pastoral ministry.

A note from the author:

Halfway through college, I began seriously considering missions. After an intense season of studying and praying about moving my life overseas, I began thinking about what it would look like. What would I actually do? Missions sounded exciting and romantic, but what would life look like when the rubber hit the road?

It took me a while to realize my daily life would look exactly how it looked like here. Choosing a vocation. Cultivating relationships. Maintaining a home. I forgot that while missions sounded exciting, it was really about the daily work. So the question remained: What did I feel called to do?

Many well-intentioned Christians ask the question, "Should I work in pastoral ministry?" Pursuing a job at a church or ministry seems like the next step if you're really serious about your faith. It's like the AP version of following Jesus, right? The most advanced way to love the Lord.

However, there are some problems with this rationale. Vocational ministry is not a bad thing, and God has certainly prepared some people for this work, as it plays an important part of flourishing churches and communities.

However, as we've learned, all dignifying work matters to God. He upholds the value of work, whether within a church build-ing or outside of it. Some work comes with more responsibility than others (Jas 3:1), but there is not one "right" or "best" way to work. Done with purpose, all work is ministry.

Although we should never discourage enthusiasm for the gospel, the Bible encourages wisdom in action (Ps 119:66). Instead of dropping everything to take a position at your local church, ask God to show you the path he is taking you on. Maybe it's pastoral ministry. Maybe it's global missions. Maybe it's both, or maybe it's neither. Take inventory and notice where you're placed, where you're skilled, and where you have influence.

Student Sur-vey Ques-tions

1. How do I realistically connect my faith and my work?

One way to realistically connect your faith and work is to think about Jesus as a blue-collar worker in his dad's carpentry shop. You can be assured that Jesus made quality tables and chairs. So, one way to connect your faith and your work is to do your work with great care and excellence after Jesus' example. In Micah 6:8 we are told what God requires of us: To do justice, love kindness, and to walk humbly with our God. If you learn about an injustice in the workplace (e.g., a co-worker being bullied), you can realistically connect your faith and your work by doing your due diligence to collect all the facts and then creatively and redemptively seek ways to bring justice to the situation.

2. How should I make decisions about my future?

As rational creatures, God calls us to make decisions about our future (Prov 16:1-9). However, we should not make decisions about our future alone. Rather, seek the counsel of others in your local church; seek others who have traveled this path before. Develop a pros and cons list and commit your decisions about the future to the Lord. As you wait, seek the Lord and his kingdom priorities (Matt 6:33). And, as you commit your plans to the Lord, remember Proverbs 16:1-9 tells us God will either establish our plans or veto our plans. And that's okay because God is good and he wants our good, so we know if he establishes or changes our plans, it is for our good and his glory.

notes

Which of these myths are you tempted to believe?
What truth does God provide to counter those
myths? Use the space below to reflect.

Don't Panic

"Cast all your anxiety on him because he cares for you."
1 Peter 5:7

PAIGE WILEY

Most students spend their college years worrying about what's coming next. What should I major in? What classes should I take next semester? Who should I live with? What internship would launch my career the right way? Most importantly, and most terrifyingly for some students: What does God want me to do with the rest of my life?

As an undecided, indecisive undergrad, this was my biggest fear. If I didn't figure out who I was going to become by the time it took me to finish a four-year degree, I was toast. Not only was I uncertain, but the fear of making a wrong decision was paralyzing.

Maybe this relates to your experience as well. According to a recent Barna study, nearly half of millennials are afraid of making the wrong career choice.[6] Our own research concluded that 91% of college students surveyed experienced some sort of worry or anxiety in making a decision about the future.[7] If you're feeling the same things, we want you to know you're not alone.

why all the worry?

I would argue that there are deeper questions hiding behind this simple one — questions about your value, worth, and identity. It's not simply "What kind of work do I want to do?" It's something more. When we dig deep, I think the real question is who am I, and what am I going to become?

If this is true, it's no wonder students are experiencing a spike in anxiety and worry. We're not just asking questions about professions, jobs, or a set of skills. Students are increasingly anxious as their careers become more tightly knit with their identity. It's not a question of what you do. It's a question of who you are.

the trend of worrying more

Without surprise, struggles with anxiety have been a growing trend for students over the past few decades. We know that school, work, and career choice are among the biggest pieces of a student's life, and with increased pressure to succeed in classes, extracurriculars, and internships, fear of failure heightens as well. Factor in the spotlight of perfect performance on social media, and it's no wonder that anxiety, worry, and fear are more mainstream.

the pressure, it seems, is on

Whether we like it or not, the world ushers us into worry as we strive to be more and more perfect. Making the right career moves, gaining the right networks, spending our time most effectively, and so on. Until we write a new narrative for our work, this is the one being written for us.

rewriting work without the worry

So let's take a step back. John 10:10 tells us that "the devil comes to steal, kill, and destroy." Second Timothy 1:7 tells us "God did not give us a spirit of fear." Worry and fear are cousins. Worry robs us of our intended joy in the Spirit. Fear steals our trust in God as sovereign and good. Worry is not of God; it is a strategy used by the evil one to "steal, kill, and destroy."

I can't speak to your experience, but I can speak to my own. When I think back to my college years, I see how worry drained me until I was devoid of joy.

Worry promised wisdom, and in return, gave me confusion.

Worry promised peace, but instead gave me anxiety.

Worry promised comfort, but in reality, clouded my vision with chaos.

Worry wasn't worth the trade-off.

the path to less worry

We know that fear and worry are obstacles to experiencing comfort and peace. But how do we learn to fight these feelings and trust Jesus in the process?

First, we must remember that our primary identity is rooted in Christ. In his work that is declared finished on the cross, we can rest in our work, knowing that it is not our works that bring us salvation, but the blood of Christ that was shed for our sins. He did the work that we could never individually do. No matter what success or failure we face in the work world, Christ is and always will be enough.

Another gift of comfort comes from Proverbs 16:9, reminding us that "humans plan their course, but the Lord establishes their steps."

We can chart our course all day long, but our lives are ultimately in the Lord's hands. To some, this may sound scary. But think about the freedom this gives us. Even with our perfect dream boards, Pinterest ideas, and 10-year-plans, there are too many unforeseen circumstances and incalculable variables. We'll never get it right on our own, and the good news is we don't have to. When we submit our anxiety about the future to the Lord, worry turns into peace, and anxiety into comfort.

Here is what Jesus says about worry in Matthew 6:26-34:

> Look at the birds of the air, they do not sow or reap or store away in barns, and yet your heavenly Father feeds them. Are you not much more valuable than they? Can any one of you by worrying add a single hour to your life? And why do you worry about clothes? See the flowers of the field grow. They do not labor or spin. Yet I tell you that not even Solomon in all his splendor was dressed like one of these. If that is how God clothes the grass of the field, which is here today and tomorrow is thrown into the fire, will he not much more clothe you - you of little faith? So do not worry, saying, 'What shall we eat?' or 'What shall we drink?' or 'What shall we wear?' For the pagans run after all these things, and your heavenly Father knows that you need them. But seek first his kingdom and righteousness, and all these things will be given to you as well. Therefore, do not worry about tomorrow, for tomorrow will worry about itself. Each day has enough trouble of its own.

These verses offer joyful submission in response to the temptation to worry. God understands your needs. He cares for you. He won't let you fall.

That being said, you are hardwired to be dependent. When we tell God, "I don't trust you; I want to plan it out myself," we are actually withholding a piece of our life that God desires to have. There's a reason life seems too difficult to figure out alone. You were created to need God, and submission to his will brings joy and peace. He wants all aspects of your life, even your work.

God understands your needs. He cares for you. He won't let you fall.

[6] *"Millennials: Big Career Goals, Limited Job Prospects."* Barna Group. Accessed April 16, 2019. https://www.barna.com/research/millennials-big-career-goals-limited-job-prospects/.
[7] Made to Flourish, *Vocational Survey*, 2019.

How do you feel when you think about your future?

Circle all that apply.

curious · cautious · optimistic

worried · happy · motivated

excited · enthusiastic · pessimistic

hesitant · uncertain · joyful

determined · anxious · hopeful

hopeless · overwhelmed · stressed

concerned · impatient · unbothered

passionate · peaceful · inadequate

exhilarated · confident · diligent

secure · insecure · frustrated

afraid · eager · confused

Reflect on the words you circled on the next page.

notes

In the word bank, did you circle more positive or negative emotions? Do you see any patterns emerge? How does the gospel speak to those emotions? Take some time to write and reflect.

"Even when you find your dream job, you're likely to see that over time, things change–you change, the market changes, and the company changes. At best, a dream job is a moving target."

Chip Roper

*"8 Myths That Can Ruin
Your Sense of Calling"*

'Life's most persistent and urgent question is 'What are you doing for others?''

—Martin Luther King Jr.[1]

Work is Service. Passion is Privilege.

PAIGE WILEY AND LUKE BOBO

You're going to hear one of two things about how to make career decisions.

First, you're going to hear people tell you to follow your passion. Chase your dreams. Achieve your goals. Pave your own way. Graduation commencements, motivational posters, and social media are riddled with messages like these. If life is about following your passion, it's up to you to find or create your own fulfillment.

You're also going to hear the opposite, that following your passion is a pipe dream. Idealism. Something nice in theory, but unrealistic.

How do we interpret these opposing worldviews? What is the biblical view of passion and work? How do we, as Christians, navigate the career path process? Let's explore together.

work is service

We've established that work is a part of God's original design. We've learned that work is intended to be good, giving us responsibility and purpose as co-cultivators with God. Although work is now subject to toil, we use it to serve God and serve our neighbors, partnering with God is the renewal of a broken Earth, day by day.

The problem is that sometimes we still view work as a service to us. Over the last few decades, Western society has shifted culturally from asking "What can my work do for my neighbor?" to "What can my work do for me? With an increasing number of majors, jobs, and online career assessments, it's no wonder we are scrambling for our place among the plethora of options. It's wise to seek a good vocational fit, but believing that finding the right job is about us — our passions, our goals, our fulfillment — misses the mark of the gospel of Christ.

So what does the gospel tell us?

Second Corinthians 5:14-15 leads us to God's heart for our vocational fit:

> For the love of Christ controls us, because we have concluded this: that one has died for all, therefore all have died; and he died for all, that those who live might no longer live for themselves but for him who, for their sake, died and was raised.

This reminds me of Matthew 16:24, where Jesus preaches a similar message:

> "Whoever wants to be my disciple must deny themselves and take up their cross and follow me."

The gospel preaches self-denial. There's something about taking on the identity of Christ that requires us to shed our own agendas. To reorder our loves: God first, everything else second. More of him, less of me. We aren't at the top of the list anymore. Therefore, our work shouldn't be used to glorify ourselves, either.

Danger of self-service, rather than service to God and neighbors, is contrary to God's design for our work. By definition, work is service. It should not be about us. It cannot be about us. If our work is about our dreams, our goals, ourselves, we're missing the point.

where does passion for work fit?

So now what? Is there room for enjoyment in work? Is pursuing passion a possibility?

Absolutely. God is a wondrous and creative God. He sculpted you as a potter forming beauty out of clay (Is 64:8). It is evident you were created with a design in mind.

This means that God created you with specialities. Gifts, talents, passions, burdens of the heart. That's one of my favorite parts about God. His craftsmanship is evident in the hearts and minds of those he created. The reason you have passions is because God created you that way.

Privilege is whether we get to use those in our everyday jobs.

If we get to fulfill our passions in the context of work, that is something to celebrate. It's a God-given joy to do the things we feel made to do but it's not guaranteed. God loves giving good gifts to his children, yet we live in a fallen and broken world. Passion is good to follow, but it cannot be everything. The key to satisfaction is not in having the right circumstances, but finding contentment where you are placed (Phil 4:12).

I'm a firm believer that the more time we spend with God, the more our hearts align with his. Therefore, the more we become like God, the more we want to serve others in our work. When we reframe our view of working to serve others instead of fulfilling our own desires, contentment comes more naturally because it's not about us.

If we know work isn't about us and God created work and our lives uniquely for certain purposes, places, and times, we need to understand the differences between both primary and secondary callings, and vocations versus occupations. As you think through decisions before you, here are a few differences between a vocation and an occupation. As Christians, we believe God calls us to certain things in certain seasons, but we also know those callings may change over time. Knowing the difference is an important piece of your work journey.

The reason you have passions is because God created you that way.

vocation or occupation: what's the difference?

A vocation and an occupation (job) are not one in the same. As Dan Doriani explains, "A job pays the bills; a calling (vocation) fits our gifts and interests." Here are two helpful definitions for vocation and occupation:

> **vocation(s):** General and specific callings from God that edify the body, enhance the world, and transcend current occupational assignments.

> **occupation(s):** Everyday labor for the glory of God and the good of others that expresses our vocation(s) while not being the full expression of our callings.

Evidence of one's specific calling is sometimes known early in life; however, for most of us, discovering one's specific calling takes many trials and errors. Keep in mind that "Whatever our specific calling, God has uniquely and divinely equipped you to perform this work assignment to his glory."

Sometimes our jobs/occupations may provide clues of our specific callings. Because of our divine design, our giftedness and talents will invariably express themselves in our jobs and occupations. Be faithful right now where God has you planted (Matt 6:33). Don't grow anxious that you might have missed or will miss your one and only chance to heed God's vocational call. God would not put that enormous pressure on you. Martin Luther said he "was less concerned that we might miss God's call to a new job or social location than that we might fail to respond obediently to the many and constant callings reaching to believers all the time." Where does God have you at this particular moment? Be faithful in this place, enjoy the journey, and trust God.

The more we become like God, the more we want to serve others in our work.

[8] Dan Doriani, *Work: It's Purpose, Dignity, and Transformation* (Phillipsburg, NJ: P&R Publishing, 2019) 69.
[9] Luke Bobo, *Living Salty and Light-filled Lives in the Workplace*, second ed. (Eugene, OR: Wipf & Stock, 2016).

Student Survey Questions

3. What if I don't know what I want to do with my life?

Too often we are told by our parents or others that we need to have our lives mapped out before graduating from high school. Some are fortunate to know what they want to do with their lives and others are not. That's okay. One thing everyone is called to do is work. So as you work and pray, allow God to reveal what he wants you to do with your life. Keep in mind, God's revealing might be sudden or it may take awhile. Use this time to experiment with different occupations and allow others to speak into your life about what you should do. Perhaps, through experimenting with different occupations and the counsel of others, God will show what to do with your life.

4. How do I turn work into worship?

Worship happens in many ways, and most of us know that worship exists outside of Sunday morning music, but how do we transition worship to our work? The biggest shift we have to make is seeing the Lord in all we do. If our work is about us, we worship ourselves. But if we are acknowledge the Lord as the One who gives us our gifts, talents, resources, and ability to contribute, we shift our thinking to him. "Whatever you do, work heartily, as for the Lord and not for men." (Colossians 3:23)

notes

PAIGE WILEY

Finding Your Calling

"The place where God calls you to is the place where your deep gladness and the world's deep hunger coincide."

—Frederick Buechner

As Christians, we have both a primary calling and a secondary calling in our lives. Our primary calling is first from the Lord. It's an invitation from a God who loves us and wants to reconnect, one that requires a response. It's choosing to put away the old life and become renewed in the life God wants to give you. It's our response to the gospel call.

Once our primary calling is answered, it deeply transforms our second. We answer the call to the environments around us, including people and places to serve God by serving the world. It's our piece in the restorative process. It's why our work greatly matters.

reframing the call

So how do you discern your secondary calling? Many people start with what they look for in a job. Good hours? Decent pay? Summers off? Opportunities for advancement? None of these are bad objectives to consider. But we might be starting in the wrong place.

If you start with the question, "What can my work do for me?" you will be disappointed. Perhaps not right away, but ultimately those pursuits will leave us empty because we are starting with a question that's about self-fulfillment. If we start here, we are serving ourselves, not God. We are going against the grain of John's attitude in John 3:30 — "[Christ] must become greater; I must become less."

Self-fulfilling questions blind us to God's purpose for work, which involves service to families, organizations, environments, and communities. If we're looking to serve ourselves first, we're doing things out of order. Instead of asking what work can do for us, we need to ask "What does the world need?"

There's no shortage of problems around the globe, so it shouldn't take long to list a few. Be vague or be specific. Pay attention to what your heart feels most burdened for.

Once you've shifted your mindset to what the world needs, follow-up with a list of things you're most passionate about. These passions can be clues to understanding what God designed you to do.

Let's break it down into two questions. As you consider these, don't limit yourself. No thought is too silly or too small to write down. Use this chance to think outside the box. Maybe even consider taking a week to track when these moments happen.

where do you feel holy contentment?
What activities bring you joy? When does time pass the quickest? In what scenarios do you feel most like yourself? What activities make you come alive?

where do you feel holy discontentment?
What riles you up? Where do you feel the most burden for the hurt and brokenness in the world? Does it have to do with broken relationships? Broken systems? What breaks your heart? What's wrong in the world that needs to be made right? Where do you reflect God's heart for justice?

what comes to mind when thinking about what the world needs?

For an extra layer of insight, call a friend, a neighbor, or a family member. Somebody who knows your heart. Ask them what passions and talents they see in you and record those notes here:

passions and talents:

This won't be a complete list, but it's a start. Some seasons of life will lengthen your lists. Others might cause you to cross things off. Treat your passions like a whiteboard, not a stone tablet. They're flexible, erasable, and ever-changing.

calling as God's design

I love thinking about work in terms of God's design. Let's take, for example, a tree. A tree has a specific design. Functions of a tree include absorbing carbon dioxide, offering shelter, and producing oxygen. If a tree were to take an inventory of its strengths and capabilities, it would have a long list to choose from. That's the mark of a good design!

Now let's imagine if that tree was asked to provide a habitat for fish, regulate water flow, or provide clean water for the surrounding ecosystem. It probably couldn't do those tasks well, because that is not how the tree was designed.

Now should the tree be distraught? Not at all. Because those actions are actually performed well by another member of the ecosystem: lakes! Lakes offer a different set of functions for a healthy and diverse environment. Both are good, bringing different strengths to the table. Another mark of excellent design.

This is exactly what Paul talks about in 1 Corinthians 12:17-20, 27:

> If the whole body were an eye, where would the sense of hearing be? If the whole body were an ear, where would the sense of smell be? But in fact God has placed the parts in the body, every one of them, just as he wanted them to be. If they were all one part, where would the body be? As it is, there are many parts, but one body. ...You are the body of Christ, and each one of you is a part of it.

Too often, we are trees trying to be lakes, or lakes trying to be trees. We become frustrated when we don't seem to function in the right fit, frustrated that we aren't doing what we were meant to do, or being who we were meant to be. It creates discontentment and frustration when our gifts and abilities are not aligning with the work we are doing, or possibly discomfort when the world values the work of lakes more than trees when both are crucial, necessary, and valuable for the flourishing of the environment around them.

The goal is not to find flawless work or perfect vocational fulfillment. We live in a chapter of the big story filled with paradoxical tension — we are no longer in a world that "once was," and not yet in a world of what "will one day be." Chasing the perfect job to fulfill your own needs will leave you restless, like "chasing after the wind" (Eccl 1:14). Yet, finding good vocational fit will give you opportunity to grow in the right type of soil — one that leads to your own flourishing and allows you to help the entire ecosystem flourish.

All that to say, you have a design. You were uniquely crafted and molded by a creative God who wants you to use those unique gifts to serve the world. In order to discover that design, let's dive into the "Wandering Map" activity.

christian challenge

church or non-profit

made to flourish

communications

dance team

36

teaching

discipleship

small
group
leader

**career
counselor**

counseling

international
studies

Paige

leadership

k-state

marching
band

south africa

**study
abroad**

WWOOF/ireland

england

anthropology

The Chaos Theory/ Wandering Map

Theory: You have no idea what will happen in 3-5 years, but you can look back on the opportunities and experiences in your life so far, as they will likely have some sort of connection.

Wandering Map: Though we may have no idea what our future will look like, but we can look back to the past and trace the (seemingly) random things to give us clues for the future. In the space below, create a map with previous jobs, past opportunities, and pivotal moments that shaped your life. After you've mapped those things out, make "threads" of connection. What are threads throughout? Does this hint at your "design?" How does the past nudge you to your future?

Let's remember, our primary calling is to God. Whether you find the perfect vocational fit or not, your primary identity rests on his unwavering foundation. Our secondary calling gives us an opportunity to respond to the first, with opportunity to serve God by serving others. It's not about us. It's not about fulfillment. It's about joining God in his project to make all things new.

notes

What are you called to? What kind of redemptive work excites you? What steps do you want to take to pursue that calling?

your wandering map

Your turn.
Create your own wandering map here.

Cultivating Virtue

LUKE BOBO

Whether you know it or not, you are participating in a social system known as the economy, and upon graduation you will continue that participation through your daily work. Your daily work — a creative service — will contribute to a "mysterious, enormous, and organic collaboration with others for the sake of the life of the world."[10]

Volitional and moral human beings are the engine behind the economy. This implies, of course, that our economy has an urgent need for virtuous workers. This need for virtuous workers begs two questions. One, "What am I becoming today?" and two, "How will I cultivate virtues such as love for God and love for neighbor?" Life and work are more than finding the right fit or settling into a comfortable place of employment. All of life requires us to "live, move, and have our being" in a virtuous way, hopefully making the world around us a little better. This only occurs, though, when we live in such a way that our responses to life, including our jobs, are virtuous, or seeking of the good, true, and beautiful in all pursuits, decisions, and actions.

formation or malformation

Workplaces, by the mere reason that we will spend more than 90,000 hours in them over our lifetimes, can form us and malform us. Even if you work remotely, you are still being formed by your work culture. So active participation in our spiritual formation is vital.

So how do we resist this tidal wave of being malformed? The Bible shows us the antidote is relentlessly and rhythmically cultivating godly virtues, for a lifetime.

God uses the workplace, along with the church, as cultivating virtue schoolhouses, to grow us into maturity. And our maturity has a goal: a maturity with a "stature measured by Christ's fullness" (Eph 4:13).

liturgical audit

Our discrete daily habits, which subversively and unconsciously become daily liturgies, reveal much about what kind of persons we are: virtuous or not virtuous. Our habits also reveal what or who we truly love and serve. Our daily habits reveal what story or cultural narrative we are living by, and they reveal who or what we truly worship.

The first step to reorder our loves and to cultivate godly virtues is to perform an inventory. Reflect on the rituals and rhythms of your life. Reflect upon your daily, weekly, monthly, and annual routines. These rituals, rhythms, and routines add up to daily, weekly, monthly, and annual liturgies. To identify these liturgies, we need to ask, "What is my vision of the good life?" Or "What are other competing cultural narratives?" Our vision of the good life and these cultural narratives fuel our liturgies.

The goal here is to uncover idols you love, serve, and therefore, worship in place of or alongside of God. Loving, serving, and worshipping idols is not benign; loving, serving, and worshipping idols shape our habits and, consequently, our loves, affections, desires, thirsts, and hungers. In short, idols malform us and we will become like them if left unchecked (Ps 115:8).

"Virtues,
quite simply,
are good
moral
habits."

—James K. A. Smith

Idolatry Inventory[11]

Identify two to three statements that might describe something you love too much, or which you derive too much of your worth from.

I only have worth if / life only has meaning if...

1. Power idolatry I have power and influence over others.
2. Approval idolatry I am loved and respected by _____.
3. Comfort idolatry I have this kind of pleasure experience, a particular quality of life.
4. Control idolatry I am able to get mastery over my life in the area of _____.
5. Helping idolatry People are dependent on me and need me.
6. Dependence idolatry Someone is there to protect me and keep me safe.
7. Independence idolatry I am completely free from obligations or responsibilities to take care of someone.
8. Work idolatry I am highly productive and getting a lot done.
9. Achievement idolatry I am being recognized for my accomplishments, and I am excelling in my work.
10. Materialism idolatry I have a certain level of wealth, financial freedom, and very nice possessions.
11. Religion idolatry I am adhering to my religion's moral codes and accomplished in its activities.
12. Individual person idolatry This one person is in my life and happy to be there, and/or happy with me.
13. Irreligion idolatry I feel I am totally independent of organized religion and am living by a self-made morality.
14. Racial/cultural idolatry My race and culture is ascendant and recognized as superior.
15. Inner ring idolatry A particular social grouping or professional grouping or other group lets me in.
16. Family idolatry My children and/or my parents are happy and happy with me.
17. Relationship idolatry Mr./Ms. Right is in love with me.
18. Suffering idolatry I am hurting, in a problem; only then do I feel worthy of love or able to deal with guilt.
19. Ideology idolatry My political or social cause is making progress and ascending in influence or power.
20. Image idolatry I have a particular kind of look or body image.

substitution: old for new

Once you have completed your personal inventory, ask, "What are the habits that support these idols?" For example, one habit that supports work idolatry (see 8) is routinely skipping a Sabbath rest. One habit that supports image idolatry (see 20) is being obsessed with fashioning and managing the most perfect and attention-getting image on Instagram.

Substitute these bad habits with virtue forming habits. And we must practice these good habits so they become like muscle memory.

There are three ways to acquire new habits/virtues. **First,** we learn virtues by entering Jesus' apprenticeship program. In Matthew 11:28-30, Jesus offers us a gracious invitation to his brand of apprenticeship or discipleship. Jesus is inviting us to follow him, to serve him, and to learn from him so that we can live freely and lightly. **Second,** we learn virtues by imitating exemplars of virtuous living. Scripture encourages us to imitate virtuous people. Consider the Apostle Paul's words to the Corinthian church, "Follow my example, as I follow the example of Christ" (1 Cor 11:1). **Third,** learning virtues takes practice because "good moral habits are like internal dispositions to the good—they are character traits that become woven into who you are so that you are the kind of person who is included to be compassionate, forgiving, and so forth."[12]

Reflect on what old habits need to be replaced with new habits. What required practices come to mind to cultivate these new habits? For example, to avoid work idolatry, routinely practice rest. To avoid image idolatry, take regular and intentional social media sabbaths. Share these practices with a friend of virtue who will keep you accountable.

We should issue a warning at this point: These new habits must be grounded in Christ, through the disciplines, to avoid falling victim to legalism or creating a form of false piety. Have a long view; establishing virtuous habits will be a lifetime journey.

Give yourself a break and be patient with this lifelong cultivation of new habits and virtues. You aren't alone in the virtue formation process. A combination of community and the Holy Spirit help us become who we are meant to be.

> These new habits must be grounded in Christ, through the disciplines, to avoid falling victim to legalism or creating a form of false piety.

[10] *For the Life of the World (FLOW) Video Curriculum,* Creative Service, Episode 3.
[11] This inventory was originally created by Tim Keller.
[12] James K. A. Smith, *You Are What You Love: The Spiritual Power of Habit* (Grand Rapids: Brazos, 2016) 16.

Student Sur-vey Ques-tions

5. How do I invest in my work without being consumed by it?

You will have many vocations in your life. As a worker, son, daughter, church member, spouse, neighbor, friend, parent, etc. The number of vocations in your life will fluctuate, but to fulfill these callings well, first learn that you have a limited supply of energy. Realizing that your paid work is only a piece of that "vocational puzzle," you can learn to prioritize your work well and find rhythms of rest. Make a list of your current vocations and seek God's wisdom in how to spend your energy and time well.

6. Is for-profit business just as "good" as non-profit work?

People often subconsciously create a hierarchy of work that bring goodness or glory to God. Ministers, missionaries, and non-profit workers are often lifted up as the "good workers" and all others fall somewhere down the scale. However, if we think about work that contributes to the common good — entrepreneurs, plumbers, educators, mechanics — we realize that all work (outside of sin) holds potential.

7. How is work good outside of evangelism?

Unfortunately, the narrative that many Christians work hear is that their work is only good for reaching the non-believers around them. We, of course, should be praying for and pursuing the people around us — believers or not. However, we often gloss over the idea that our work is inherently good. When you go to work, are you helping people in some way? Are you organizing, cultivating, stewarding, developing, teaching, training, or growing the world around you? Those good things mirror the characteristics of a good God. Therefore, your work is "good."

notes

What comes to mind when you hear the words "the good life" and what does that look like?

Diaries of a Career Counselor

PAIGE WILEY

I had the privilege to be a career counselor in college. My job was to help undecided students explore options in majors, careers, and vocational goals. I administered aptitude tests, revised resumes, and helped weigh educational options. I got to meet people at their most excited and most vulnerable. I got to see the carefully woven tapestry of each person's values, talents, and gifts, seeing their eyes light up as they talked about the things they cared for most. I got to meet people on the path to who they wanted to become. Basically it was a pretty cool job.

Eventually, going to work was one of my favorite ways to worship. To be on the receiving end of listed passions, interests, dreams, and ideas showed me again and again the diversity of God's design. "I want to help people," was the most common desire, each with a different blueprint for what that could look like. It was apparent there was something in the human spirit that longed to make the world a better place, whether through organizing, crafting, building, or cultivating. To me, it clearly spoke to our intentioned desire to join God's restoration for a broken world. There's something in us — each one of us — that longs to "use our powers for good."

Being a career counselor allowed me to daily witness this intersection of power and passion, but my hope is that the church will learn to celebrate this as well. There's something beautiful about seeing each person as a unique masterpiece, cheering on their visions, talents, and goals. There's something beautiful about each person having a part to play; whether in a musical, an assembly line, or an office. There's a craft to God's design, in that he uniquely created each one of us with a different task to do. But it's the weaving of these things together that makes us the body of Christ.

Now What?

Our biggest goal in creating this workbook is to show you the freedom you have in the pursuit of work. It's a freedom that originates in the creation story, a freedom that is reiterated in the gospel story, and a freedom that is emulated in the daily work of diligent Christ followers every day.

Sometimes, serving God through our work looks like becoming a pastor. Sometimes, it means pursuing a career in overseas missions. But we are all missionaries on Monday. Whether you become a welder, a teacher, a sales agent, a forester, a librarian, a technician, a lawyer, an electrician, a CEO, or a stay at home parent, your work matters. Whatever you do, you were made with freedom in mind. The world doesn't just need your work, but it needs your virtuous work for the good of your neighbor and the glory of God.

Let us leave you with a benediction, trusting the Lord will lead you and guide you in his love and steadfast nature in the next steps of life:

> 'May the favor of the Lord our God rest upon us; establish the work of our hands for us — yes, establish the work of our hands.'
>
> **Psalm 90:17**

For Additional Reading

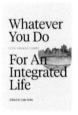

Luke Bobo, Ed.
Whatever You Do: Six Foundations for an Integrated Life.
Overland Park: Made to Flourish, 2019.

Tim Keller
Every Good Endeavor: Connecting Your Work to God's Work.
New York: Penguin Random, 2016.

Bill Burnett and David J. Evans
Designing Your Life: How to Build a Well-Lived, Joyful Life.
New York: Penguin Random, 2016.

Tom Nelson
Work Matters: Connecting Sunday Worship to Monday Work.
Wheaton: Crossway, 2011.

Kevin DeYoung
Just Do Something: A Liberating Approach to Finding God's Will.
Chicago: Moody, 2009.

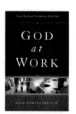

Gene Veith
God at Work: Your Christian Vocation in All of Life.
Wheaton: Crossway, 2002.

About the Authors

Luke Bobo

Luke Bobo serves as director of strategic partnerships for Made to Flourish, and brings leadership to responding to and seeking new opportunities to bring our content and training to partners, including cities, churches, organizations, and denominations.

Luke brings a rich blend of experience to Made to Flourish, having worked for 15 years in the marketplace as an engineer before pursuing an M.Div. and Ph.D., and eventually serving as the executive director of the Francis Schaeffer Institute at Covenant Seminary.

Luke recently spent time as a professor of religious studies at Lindenwood University, and wrote curriculum for a workplace ministry. Luke is a visiting instructor of contemporary culture at Covenant Seminary. He also serves as a visiting professor for Cru's Institute of Biblical Studies (IBS). He is also the author of *Living Salty and Light Filled Lives in the Workplace, A Layperson's Guide to Biblical Interpretation: A Means to Know the Personal God,* and *Race, Economics and Apologetics: Is There A Connection?*

Paige Wiley

Paige Wiley serves as the engagement coordinator at Made to Flourish. She completed the Kansas City Fellows Program in 2019, a nine month hands-on program exploring the integration of faith and work with recent college graduates. She now helps pastors engage with similar ideas through a range of diverse content and resources.

Paige worked as a career counselor for three years during her time at Kansas State University, where she became interested in God's design for each person's unique set of talents, skills, and gifts, and how to answer questions about calling and career with a biblical worldview.

Paige brings a wide range of experiences to the table, including retail work at Walt Disney World, customer service at a Parks and Recreation Department, human resources at a YMCA camp, youth programming in a South African township, and gardening in Northern Ireland.

About Made to Flourish

Made to Flourish empowers a growing network of pastors and their churches to integrate faith, work, and economic wisdom for the flourishing of their communities. From Boston to Silicon Valley, Made to Flourish has a local presence in 27 cities around the United States.

As an organization we believe God created work for the good of our neighbors and for his glory as we reflect him in our daily jobs. Whether you work in an office, at home, or somewhere in between, your work matters.

Join us as we continue to resource and equip a growing network of churches, pastors, and leaders around the country.

Get involved at madetoflourish.org.

Acknowl-edgements

Several long-suffering souls reviewed a rough draft of this book, giving us valuable feedback. We're thankful for Rachel Irons, Kris Fernhout, Kevin Rauckman, and Caleb Bobo. Your collective "eyes" on and attentiveness to this workbook, we believe, has made it better. Special thanks to our managing editor, RuthAnne Irvin, whose editing and organizing acumen was invaluable.

We also want to give acknowledgement to the students behind these thoughtful questions and relevant topics. If it weren't for your inquisitiveness, curiosity, and desire to glorify God in all that you do, we wouldn't have been inspired to write these pages. Thank you for your contribution to this work.

To quote the kind and true words of beloved TV character, Leslie Knope: "It's a lesson I've learned over and over again, but it bears repeating: No one achieves anything alone."

Made
to Flourish

Made in the USA
Columbia, SC
27 September 2022

67854209R00031